REMINGTON
and RUSSELL

Frederic Remington – One of a series of drawings
published in *Century*, *Colliers* and *Cosmopolitan*,
1889-1906, depicting the 10th US Cavalry in the West
(Library of Congress)

Charles M Russell

Return of the Horse Thieves (detail)

1900, watercolor, 21″×9″
(C M Russell Museum, Great Falls, MT)

REMINGTON and RUSSELL

Leonard Everett Fisher

GALLERY BOOKS
An imprint of W.H. Smith Publishers Inc.
112 Madison Avenue
New York, New York 10016   [c1985]
A Bison Book

Right: *Frederic Remington*

Riding Herd in the Rain

nd, wash drawing
(Buffalo Bill Historical Center, Cody, WY)

Published by Gallery Books
A Division of W H Smith Publishers Inc.
112 Madison Avenue
New York, New York 10016

Produced by
Bison Books Corp.
17 Sherwood Place
Greenwich, CT 06830

ISBN 0-8317-7375-8

Printed in Hong Kong

1 2 3 4 5 6 7 8 9 10

The Fireboat

1918, oil on canvas,
14½″×23¼″
(C M Russell Museum,
Great Falls, MT)

INTRODUCTION (1880)

In 1880, two driven young men with a thirst for rough, breezy adventure left the warm comforts of civilized America and headed for the Wild West.

Four years had passed since Colonel George Armstrong Custer and a column of the 7th Cavalry, United States Army, were massacred by the Sioux and Cheyenne at the Little Big Horn River in Montana, 25 June 1876. Not long after that fatal day, America celebrated its centennial. A month later, ex-lawman 'Wild Bill' Hickock was murdered in Deadwood, a raucous town in the Dakotas. William Frederick 'Buffalo Bill' Cody had long since killed 4000 buffaloes to feed the famished laborers laying track for the transcontinental railroad. By 1880, Boot Hill Cemetery in Dodge City, Kansas, was brimming over with the graves of gunfighters hastily buried with their boots on. Wyatt Earp and his brothers had not yet shot it out with desperadoes at the OK Corral in Tombstone, Arizona. And the Apache chieftain, Geronimo, was still on the loose, terrorizing the rest of Arizona.

The young men did not know each other, but both possessed uncommon artistic flair. They liked to draw, paint, write and one of them modelled in wax. Neither thought of themselves as accomplished artists or writers, let alone professionals. Nonetheless, the urge to communicate visually and verbally had been strong in them since early childhood. Equally as strong in both, if not overwhelming, was a desire to be free in the great outdoors.

One of them was Charles Marion Russell, 16 years old, a native of St Louis, Missouri. The other was 19-year-old Frederic Remington of Canton, New York. Each of them had his private reasons for going West. None of these were artistic in the beginning. In the end, however, Remington and Russell would leave an extraordinary historical record of a special time and place on the American scene via their painting, drawing, writing and, to a lesser degree, their sculpture. Their legacy of art and literature dealing with the quality of life on the American frontier for nearly half a century – 1880-1926 – would be so complete and penetrating as to form a permanent atmospheric knowledge of the Old West as it actually was before the heavy hand of civilization changed it. They implanted a sense of being there in our historical minds; of bearing witness to the truth of the Old West and its passing.

In any event, for nearly 50 years – since before the first salvo of the Civil War traumatized the nation, tearing it apart – small numbers of the American population had been steadily pushing back the frontier everywhere beyond the Mississippi River. By mid-century, 'Go west, young man' was the often-heard dictum aimed at the unemployed of New York City, for the most part. Why idle life away in the East when there were fortunes to be made in western gold, silver, timber, cattle, sheep, mules, farming and railroads? The inauguration of coast-to-coast rail service, New York to California, on 15 May 1869, made it all that much more possible, that much more attainable. The phrase, 'Go west, young man,' coined in 1851 by John Soule, an Indiana journalist, and later popularized by Horace Greeley in his weekly literary magazine, *The New Yorker*, was the nation's starting gun for massive westward migration, a race for opportunity and wealth. It was high in the consciousness of spirited America. And nineteenth century America, expanding inexorably toward its great vision of power and plenty through continental consolidation, was now a land whose vitality, fueled by ambition and monumental energy, was unlike that of any other country in the world. Caught up in Soule's advice and his own enthusiasm, Horace Greeley took himself west in 1870 and founded a small town in Colorado called Union Colony. A grateful citizenry later renamed the place Greeley.

To Frederic Remington, like most young men of the time, Soule's advice to go west must have entered his stream of thought with a ring of excitement and good sense. Remington was hardly unemployed or destitute. He had just inherited a modest sum of money upon the recent death of his father, Seth Remington, a newspaper publisher. At 19, Frederic Remington had little else on his mind than to abandon what he considered a stuffy Yale education, continue with his drawing and painting, marry Eva Caten and lead a vigorous outdoor life. Despite the small inheritance, Eva's father was not impressed with

Frederic's restlessness and artistic inclinations. Artists and writers had questionable prospects. They usually offered little financial stability in an uncertain world. In short, artists and writers were unreliable, and Frederic Remington seemed to have all the markings of unreliability.

Remington himself agreed and viewed his own future as dim. He decided to improve his situation, impress his would-be-father-in-law, and give Mr Caten ample reason to allow his daughter to be Mrs Frederic Remington. He would go west! He would make his fortune somehow. He would return with all the necessary prerequisites – money and property – to marry Eva Caten. Nothing like that happened. Remington, obviously, did indeed go west. Fortune eluded him, however. Instead of offering up its wealth to the aspiring Remington, the West, like a giant, powerful magnet, drew him further and further into its seasons of high adventure. Mesmerized by what he now believed to be his natural habitat, Remington decided to record it all with pen and brush, a decision that would lead him to both fame and fortune. Remington returned east a couple of years later. He had lost most of his inheritance in an ill-fated business venture calculated to produce the fortune. He was nearly flat broke but not quite. He had bought a tiny house on the Missouri River. Yet, the only solid link he had with his future now lay in his ever increasing portfolio of sketches. He managed to marry Eva Caten anyway, with Mr Caten's blessings, surprisingly enough. He and Eva would now try the West together in another try for the fortune.

Charles Russell was of a different stripe. Young Charlie had neither fortune, fame or females on his 16-year-old mind. Instead, he had a desperate longing to shed the encroachment of civilization. The nation was on the move. It was going West now in ever-increasing numbers, not only by horse and wagon train, but by rail as well. St Louis was a boisterous center of all this activity. Fanning out to the West were the innocents, genuinely seeking a golden future in a Promised Land for themselves and their families. Here, too, were the freebooters, ruthless and ready to wrench power and money out of the anarchy and lawlessness they promoted. Nearby were all the tough lawmen cooling tempers, allaying fears and generally trying to keep the Old West lawful and steady. And here were those who would claim from a land already spoken for by untold generations of Indians what rightfully was not theirs to claim. They were gamblers all, courageous, full of bravado, morality, immorality, malice, God, greed, goodness and ingenuity. In front of them and all around was the Army sent to its lonely outposts to make way for and protect the onrush of civilization – of conquest – moving out of the East.

Charlie Russell was none of these. In its romantic fervor, Charlie Russell's dream to go west overrode every consideration of his young life. Like Remington, school held no interest for him. And like Remington, he was something of a loner. And very early he had caught the spirit of moving freely in a pure, open and untrampled environment – albeit a near wilderness – hoping against hope that he and it could remain one, joined together forever. Charlie's reasons were all pure aesthetics. For him, the West was a natural paradise put there by the Almighty. It was not meant to be tampered with, rearranged or sullied by men and their machinery.

'Those Indians have been living in heaven for a thousand years,' he would write, 'and we took it away from 'em . . .' Charlie's written and spoken words were one in the same – sincere and right out of the saddle.

If Charlie Russell had a single ambition other than to protect and preserve the West from civilization and certain ruin, it was to live off the land as a natural part of it. His reach for a livelihood did not go much further than his horse, his paintbox and his writing pad. He was as much a cowboy as he was an artist. Some would say that his ability to communicate such deep feelings about the West made him a philosopher as well. 'Any man that can make a living doing what he likes is lucky. And I am that.'

In that year, 1880, the United States comprised 38 states. Arizona, Idaho, Montana, New Mexico, the Dakotas, Oklahoma, Utah, Washington, Wyoming, Hawaii and Alaska were all Territories. With the exception of Hawaii and Alaska, which became states after World War II, these Territories would all be admitted into the Union between 1889 and 1912. Remington and Russell converged on great tracts of this vast region as its essence was being consigned to a bygone age. They were not the first artists to ride into the West, nor would they be the last. But none would communicate through their art such first-hand reality that only participants in events can engender as these two. They were engaged in depicting a fading history. Although the Old West is gone, it remains alive and visual, secure in the art of Frederic Remington and Charles Marion Russell.

INTRODUCTION

Downing in Nigh Leader 1907, oil on canvas, 30″×50″ (*Museum of Western Art, Denver, CO*)

FREDERIC REMINGTON (1861-1909)

The artistic and literary response of Frederic Remington to the Great Plains, to the blistering heat of the Southwest, to the night chill in the Rockies, to hostile Indians, edgy troopers, leathery cowboys, nervous horses and the general ordeal of life in the open, seemed as natural to him as the environs of his New Rochelle, New York, studio. Jammed with western artifacts, symbols and memorabilia, Remington's New York studio was his West in the East. There, in his studio, far from the land he preferred, Remington recreated in paint his western self. His enthusiasm for the violence of existence in the American West never waned. It underwrote the high level of action found in his art. What emerged in all those painted actions was not only an image and spirit of the West, but the essence of the artist.

'You have struck a note of grim power,' wrote an admirer, then Secretary of the Navy Theodore Roosevelt, in November 1897. Roosevelt, an energetic advocate of the outdoor life, knew what he was writing about. He himself had experienced and relished the rawness of the West on many an adventurous trip.

Perhaps lurking deep in Remington's mind was an indelible impression made upon a small boy's imagination by his father, a Civil War veteran. Such images gave shape and form to the romance of manhood as perceived in post-Civil War America. The elder Remington had temporarily abandoned his newspaper to answer the Congressional call for a fighting army in 1861. Commissioned a Lieutenant Colonel, he rode off to war in command of the 11th New York Cavalry. He returned home and to his newspaper at the end of the war, a battle-scarred veteran whose front line experiences dazzled the fertile brain of his four-year-old son. The awesome and authentic exploits of his direct contact with history were seen and understood by Frederic as one of those rugged conflicts in life that test one's manhood. And the impetuous young Remington begged to be tested.

Canton, New York, was a small town some 25

Frederic Remington in his studio
(Remington Art Museum, Ogdensburg, NY)

or 30 miles from the Canadian border. It was about as far north in New York State and as far removed from the artistic arenas of Philadelphia, New York City, and Boston as it was distant from the western reaches of the United States. Frederic Remington was born in Canton on 1 October 1861.

From his earliest days in school, Remington showed little interest in academic routines. He was anxious to get outside. He squirmed in his seat, marking up books and papers with pencil sketches of horses and soldiers, for the most part. School cramped his vitality. He strained at these confinements. Remington was a burly, restless youngster, broader and stronger than most boys his age. A muscular swimmer, he also knew his way around horses by the time he was a teenager. Horses would remain a lifetime interest. A first class horseman, Remington would track down and closely study numerous breeds wherever his travels took him, and he traveled not only over every back trail in the West, but in southern Canada, northern Mexico, Europe and North Africa, among other places.

Remington craved the outdoors in any weather and preferred the freedom of the open air to the boredom of the schoolroom. He annoyed his teachers and parents with his continuous indifference to learning in the accepted and proper school manner. He behaved regularly like a straining colt, checked and reined in, but eager to break free and run with the wind. Young Remington's restlessness finally became intolerable. In 1874, thinking that 13-year-old Frederic needed discipline, his parents enrolled him in a military academy. As much as he admired the trappings of the military – uniforms, weapons, horses, and rugged encampments, as evidenced by all his youthful doodling – Remington was horrified by the discipline. He fled the place, was quickly found, disciplined for running away and gradually overcame his unruliness to become a popular member of the establishment. By the time he graduated, at the age of 17, he was not quite six feet tall but weighed close to 200 pounds. At 29 he would tip the scale at 230 pounds. 'There is nothing poetical about me,' he would write.

Remington's graduation from the Highland Military Academy in 1878 was uneventful. Apart from the fact that he was a good athlete, an avid reader, a fine horseman and an incorrigible sketcher, from any academic perspective his school career was undistinguished. Sketching, interestingly enough, was a desirable talent to have if one was entertaining a military career. Freehand drawing courses had long been part of the curriculum of the United States Military Academy at West Point. One can still view there examples of landscape sketches by such notable alumni as General Ulysses S Grant. A soldier who could sketch with some accuracy a target area could provide vital information. Today, photography and very sophisticated sensing devices have changed all that. But in Remington's time, ability to sketch the outdoors in a non-interpretative way was a military asset.

Being a soldier was not Frederic Remington's notion of a career, however. While still in military school he toyed with the idea of becoming a newspaperman like his father. Good books, literature and intelligent conversation were always part of the Remington household. At one point he had applied for admission to Cornell with journalism in mind. Yet, Remington always talked a great deal about studying art.

'I mean to study for an artist anyhow . . .,' he wrote an uncle in the spring of his graduation from the Highland Military Academy.

Finally, Remington made a decision. He turned his sights on art. Instead of Cornell, he entered the freshman class at Yale University in New Haven, Connecticut. New Haven was the place to be in 1878. The first commercial telephone exchange in America began operating there in January, but, more importantly, Yale boasted the only university level professional art school in the country.

Once again academia depressed Remington. The Yale University School of Fine Arts, established only seven years before Remington's arrival, offered little else but endless hours of drawing from classical plaster casts. Bored beyond endurance but not quite ready to give up Yale, Remington headed for the outdoors again.

While barely tolerating the art school and its stifling routine, he entered the university's sporting arenas with predictable gusto. He found the needed challenge in contact sport rather than dead white plaster casts recreated from the ruins of ancient Greek and Roman figures. And nothing was more aggressively appropriate as a manly activity than the 'sport' of boxing, a questionable activity in those years. Boxing was illegal in many places, public or private. Boxing gloves were fairly new but optional. Boxing itself would not become popular until well into the 1880s when John L Sullivan became the bare-knuckle heavyweight champion of the world and invited all comers to dethrone him. But bare knuckle or not, Remington hammered his opponents with quick fists and proved to be a skillful fighter.

In addition, his need to be physical coupled with his boundless energy and enthusiasm led him straight to football. His size and quickness – his zest for head-knocking and bone-crushing contact – made him an outstanding varsity player at Yale. Remington was a member of the team captained by the legendary Walter Chauncey Camp, the 'father of American football,' and the originator of the All American teams.

Remington's second year at Yale was nearing an end when in 1880 his father died. Suddenly, life took on a different twist and meaning for the restless Remington. His inheritance, however small, was enough to set him in motion; to whet his appetite for life beyond the university. His mother's ambitions for him – that he remain at Yale, graduate like most normal people of his station, and secure a reasonable position in a secure profession – went unheeded. He left Yale, met Eva Caten and faced his future. The die was cast. He would go West.

Remington's arrival in the West was something close to a homecoming. Although his previous travel was limited to New York and New England, his sense of belonging to this new place was immediate. It mattered little whether he was sharing a campfire with a weary cowhand, eating dust while galloping with the cavalry, relaxing with saloonkeepers, or befriending grizzly prospectors, trappers, or suspicious Indians. Fearless and compulsive, he threw himself into this hostile environment as if he had been born in the shadow of the nearest mesa. His likeable enthusiasm made friends for him everywhere, and his facility with horses made him accepted in the company of high-ranking army officers like General Nelson Appleton Miles who conducted the military campaigns against the Indians, and the ordinary anonymous cowboy.

Remington charged into his new world and explored every rock, river, stream and hill from the snow-tipped Rockies in the north to the baking deserts of the southwest. He was the complete rugged western individual, comfortable on his horse and as handy with a rope, pistol and rifle as the most intrepid, weather-beaten cowhand or US Cavalry Trooper. What made him different was his inquisitiveness and eagerness to learn everything there was to know about the West as quickly as possible. He badgered everyone he met as if he was trying to make up for the first 20 years of his life having had the misfortune of being born in the East. What made him a cut above the rest was his sketchpad and artistic perceptions of time, place and history.

Always the artist, Remington would write, 'The scouts, packers, and teamsters add artistic qualities in their strongly molded faces . . . that the most casual onlooker could not perceive.'

Once in a while he would try to remember that he came West to make a quick fortune and return home to Eva Caten, but the spell of the West and the compulsion to set it all down pictorially drove him further and further away from his original intent. Late in 1881, having explored the area for the better part of a year, he sent a clumsy sketch drawn on wrapping paper to the editors of Harper's Weekly in New York. The sketch dealing with Arizona cowboys had to be redrawn by a more knowledgeable and polished draftsman for publication. But the Harper's Weekly editors thought the sketch so interesting a subject for its readership that they decided to use it. Redrawn by W A Rogers 'from a sketch by

Frederic Remington,' it appeared in the 25 February 1882 issue of the magazine.

The appearance of the sketch and his name in print together with Rogers in one of the most prestigious publications in the East did not bring Remington his fortune. Get-rich-quick schemes continued to drift in and out of his mind. Finally, after crisscrossing and sketching the region from Canada to Mexico, riding miles of the Oregon Trail as it passed through Fort Laramie and South Pass in Wyoming and roaming the environs of the Santa Fe Trail from Independence, Missouri to Santa Fe, New Mexico, Remington bought a mule-raising ranch. The small spread was close to the City of Kansas (it would become Kansas City in 1889), Missouri. Withing weeks, he knew that he was not cut out to be a mule raiser. He sold the ranch at a loss – Remington was hardly a business operator – bought a modest house in the City of Kansas, and took to the high roads and back trails with his sketchpad, determined to make a living with his art. The selling of his sketch to Harper's Weekly was strong encouragement. The making and selling of his pictures, was to Remington, within the realm of possibility.

Remington went out among his favorite creatures: soldiers, cowhands, Indians and horses. He filled his pads with sketches and returned to the house in the city of Kansas from time to time to redraw and polish the visual notes he had made in the field. For a time he sold a few of these, but not enough to renew his dwindling bank account. The little cash he had left was fast disappearing. Moreover, Remington was not as sure-handed as he thought he was or would like to be. However much he believed himself to be an artistic self-taught loner, he was beginning to feel that he needed some improvement. It was time to go East.

He returned to New York thinking more of Eva, marriage and how to improve his bank account than artistic improvement. Back home in New York, he assured Eva, his mother, and most of all Eva's father, that there was still a fortune to be made somewhere in the West. Remington could not let it go. The struggle would bring success. But the struggle had to be in the West. Convinced, and knowing full well that nothing could dissuade the stubborn Remington, Eva Caten's father gave his blessings to their marriage.

Soon after the young couple were married, they returned to Remington's small house in the City of Kansas. With characteristic enthusiasm, Remington threw himself into his picture-

Trooper in Tow

(Library of Congress)

their small house, most of the cattle, once driven into town from points along the 780 mile Santa Fe Trail by weary, grimy cowboy drovers, were beginning to be shipped by rail. The mechanics of industry were starting to be felt in the gateways to the West and Southwest. Nevertheless, the City of Kansas was still the unpaved host of the whooping, hollering, hard drinking cattlemen, who conveyed their beasts by trail and rail from the great open spaces of the Southwest to the auction stalls and abattoirs of the City of Kansas in Missouri.

Few in the City of Kansas and other centers of population nearby were interested in art, let alone in Frederic Remington's pictures. He sold few, and for Frederic and Eva, things began to slide from bad to worse. Eva returned to New York while Frederic, determined to strike it rich for them both, remained behind for one more chance — a chance to find gold, literally.

With Eva gone, Remington joined a couple of shaggy prospectors who were on their way into the Arizona Territory, a place alive with renegade Apaches. The Chiricahua Apaches under the leadership of Geronimo had been fighting a guerrilla war with white Americans for years. Remington's own description of the Apache character is blunt:

'. . . they are cruel, one does not have to look a second time to guess; he does not have to see them torture a rabbit as a pastime, for the subdued ferocity of the tiger is in their eyes and gleams out savagely . . .'

For the next nine or 10 months, Remington prospected for gold in Arizona and Texas, sketching everywhere he went. His saddlebags were crammed with drawings of western life as he ran headlong into it. At one point on his wanderings he and his two prospecting partners were surprised by Apaches. But until they were convinced of their peaceful intent and had left with a sack of flour, Remington and his friends spent a sleepless night.

'. . . to my unbounded astonishment and consternation there sat three Apaches on the opposite side of our fire with their rifles across their laps. My comrades . . . positively gasped in amazement . . . and although we had been previously very sleepy, we now sat up and entertained our guests until they stretched themselves out . . . During that night I never closed my eyes . . .'

Eventually, Remington returned to the City of Kansas safe and sound but without an ounce of gold. He had plenty of sketches, however, but little money. He was broke with just enough

making career with unabashed confidence. He would sell what he would create on paper. Tucked away in some small recess of his brain and never too far from the surface was the urge to find a good money-making venture enabling him to devote his life to the West, to putting it all down on paper and canvas, and to Eva.

All that was easier dreamed and done. The City of Kansas was a rugged place for honeymooners in 1883, especially for the inexperienced Eva Remington. The City of Kansas, Missouri, lay on the eastern banks of the Missouri River, a link of the Santa Fe Trail between its termini of Independence, Missouri, and Santa Fe, New Mexico. Kansas City, Kansas, directly opposite on the western side of the river, was hardly a thriving city in 1883. In fact, it was not until 1886 that Kansas City became a municipal entity by that name when the towns of Wyandotte, Armourdale, and Armstrong incorporated as one. In any event, the city of Kansas, as the young Remingtons knew it, was a major cattle market for the herds coming up the Santa Fe and Chisholm Trails from east and west Texas, New Mexico and Oklahoma. It was the largest such market in the United States.

By the time the Remingtons had moved into

The Bronco Buster

c. 1905, bronze, 32½″ × high
(The Metropolitan Museum of Art, New York, NY.
Bequest of Jacob Ruppert, 1939)

Opposite:

The Old Stagecoach of the Plains

1901, oil on canvas, 40¼″ × 27¼″
(Amon Carter Museum, Fort Worth, Texas)

dollars to get him back to New York.

Eva met him upon his return to New York City. They remained there for a while on borrowed money. Remington, meanwhile, studied figure drawing at the Art Students League in a long-delayed effort to improve his art.

In 1885, 24-year-old Frederic Remington struck pay dirt, as it were. *Harper's Weekly* bought another one of his pictures and published it in their 9 January 1886 issue. All during that year – 1886 – *Harper's* continued to publish his drawings. All of these were re-engraved for reproduction from Remington's original ink wash drawings. And this time only the name of Frederic Remington appeared. Drawings like *The Apaches are Coming* published in *Harper's* 30 January 1886 were hardly the work of a well tutored and experienced professional illustrator – and that is what these drawings were, illustrations – story telling pictures, anecdotal and aimed at objective realism as opposed to an interpretive, subjective view of someone's notion of reality. These early pictorial efforts were stiff and self conscious, if not artistically naive. They were void of linear flow, the anatomy was poor, as was the communication of solid form. A hand

cut off by a tail; a foot hidden behind a bent knee indicated that some seasoning was in order. There is accuracy in the details of the rider's gear, the construction of house and well, and in the clothing. Unfortunately such detail and its accurate communication does not make a work of art. Still, there is a certain dynamism to these rude beginnings that hint of the refinement and drama to come. A comparison between the 1886 *Coming of the Apaches* and *Roasting the Christmas Beef* published by *Harper's* 24 December 1892, indicates how far Remington would travel artistically in only six years.

Not long after *Harper's* published its January 1886 issues with the Remington drawings, other illustration commissions began to arrive with some regularity. *Harper's Weekly* continued to publish Remington over the next 10 years or more. But other periodicals, *St Nicholas*, a children's magazine, and *Outing*, a magazine edited by a onetime Yale friend, kept him busy with a variety of stories in need of illustrations.

In 1888, Remington found himself back in the West once again to his absolute and utter delight. *Century* magazine was interested in the quality of Indian life in the Southwest. More specifically,

From "*A Scout with the Buffalo Soldiers,*" written and illustrated by Frederic Remington (who is shown second in the column), *Century Magazine*, April 1889.
(*Peter Newark's Western Americana*)

the editors were interested in illustrated accounts of Indian life on the reservations.

This trip west must have been a comforting note in Remington's effort to find himself. For one thing, he left Eva happily at home in a large Manhattan apartment, though no doubt somewhat suffocated by his immense collection of cowboy gear, souvenirs and the Indian memorabilia he had been amassing since 1880. Moreover, the Remingtons were no longer without funds. Remington had been fulfilling illustration commissions as fast as he could manage them. There was money in the bank. He was no longer chasing a pot of gold at the end of the western rainbow on this trek. This was a bona fide assignment.

Remington spent the summer with the 10th United States Cavalry in the heat of the Arizona Desert. Much to his liking, he accompanied the US Army Apache Scouts looking for warring Chiracahua and White Mountain Apaches not on Indian reservations. Although caught up in the excitement of such adventure, Remington never let physicality and his enthusiasm for such activity diminish his artistic perceptions and sensitivity.

'A traveler in the valley,' he wrote earlier, 'looking up at the squatting forms of men against the sky, would have remembered the great strength of chiaroscuro in some of [Gustave] Dore's drawings and to himself have said that this was very like it.'

Remington baked in the dry heat the whole summer long. The riding was hard, the living was harder, and sudden violent death became a near indifferent expectation. Remington struggled through it all. His endurance was being stretched to the limit and he was admittedly out of shape, blaming his aches on the 'effeminacy of the studio.'

Back in his New York studio, far from the discomfort of life in the open, Remington reworked his on-the-spot sketches and transcribed them into more polished drawings and paintings. Some of these works found their way to the large public exhibitions of the National Academy of Design on Fifth Avenue and the American Watercolor Society.

Needless to say, the general public was awed by Remington's dynamic revelations of an area of America that offered such adventure and strange beauty, a violent and savage place of awesome nature. Most of those who visited the Remington paintings and kept abreast of his published illustrations and writings would never see the region. Yet, they responded to Remington's experience with intense interest if not romantic yearnings that bordered on their own western fantasies. Whatever, the audience for Frederic Remington was widening.

As the year moved along, Remington spent long hours in his comfortable studio painting, writing drawing and sculpting. In 1895 he published a novel, Pony Tracks. Three years later this was followed by another novel, Crooked Trails. In February of that same year 1898, the battleship USS Maine blew up in Havana Harbor. By April, the United States and Spain were at war. Publisher William Randolph Hearst sent Remington to cover the war with his pen and brush. The war was over in July when Cuba was secured by American forces and Puerto Rico fell to American troops commanded by Remington's old western acquaintance, General Nelson Appleton Miles.

With the war over, Remington quickly headed for his studio and its familiar surroundings. The commissions came rapidly. Collier's Weekly magazine reproduced Remington paintings in full color made possible by new technology. In 1902, there was another novel, John Ermine of Yellowstone. The book became a popular play produced in Boston, Chicago and New York. From time to time, Remington produced book illustrations. He had illustrated Francis Parkman's Oregon Trail in 1900, and in 1902, he illustrated President Theodore Roosevelt's Ranch Life and the Hunting Trail.

As his writing continued, his paintings grew stronger and began to encompass with brilliant color and draftsmanship not only the ordeal of life in the fading Old West, but the essence of life itself as it existed in a raw natural environment. These weren't soldiers shooting Indians and vice versa, or cowhands riding herd in the loneliness of a wet night. It was man against man; man against nature; and if you will, nature against man. The cruelty of white conquest of the Indian was all there. But implicit in all these images is the enormity of the human struggle. In such later paintings as Fight for the Waterhole, A Taint in the Wind, The Luckless Hunter and Apache Medicine Song. Remington began to introduce a note of melancholia. Perhaps it was his own longing for a passing age which he documented so well; or a ripening of his own spirit.

This will never be known. Nor will the artistic and esthetic realms Frederic Remington would have moved his art and his devotees if he had lived a little longer.

After a brief illness, Frederic Remingon died 26 December 1909. He was only 48 years old.

The Night Herder

nd, oil on board,
12⅛″×18″
(*Buffalo Bill
Historical Center,
Cody, WY*)

A Dash for the Timber

1889, oil on canvas, 48¼″ × 84⅛″
(Amon Carter Museum, Fort Worth, TX)

The Scout: Friends or Enemies?

c. 1890, oil on canvas, 27″×40″
(Sterling and Francine Clark Art Institute, Williamstown, MA)

Preceding spread:

Cavalry in an Arizona Sandstorm

c. 1889, oil on canvas, 22⅛″×35¼″
(Amon Carter Museum, Fort Worth, TX)

27

Aiding A Comrade

c. 1890, oil on canvas, 34″×48″
(The Hogg Brothers Collection, Museum of Fine Arts, Houston, TX)

The Buffalo Hunt

1890, oil on canvas,
34″×49″
(*Buffalo Bill Historical
Center, Cody, WY*)

The Sun Dance

1890, oil on canvas,
40″×27″
(Remington Art
Museum, Ogdensburg,
NY)

Captured

1899, oil on canvas, 27″×40⅛″ (Sid Richardson Collection of Western Art, Fort Worth, TX)

Following spread:

Charge of the Rough Riders at San Juan Hill

1899, oil on canvas, 35″×60″ (Remington Art Museum, Ogdensburg, NY)

A Reconnaissance

1902, oil on canvas,
27″×40⅛″
(Amon Carter Museum,
Fort Worth, TX)

Following spread:

The Emigrants

1904, oil on canvas,
30″×45″
(The Hogg Brothers
Collection, Museum of
Fine Arts, Houston, TX)

The Last March

1906, oil on canvas, 30″×22″
1906, oil on canvas, 30″×22″
(Remington Art Museum, Ogdensburg, NY)

Preceding spread:

Pony Tracks in the Buffalo Trails

1904, oil on canvas, 30¼″×51¼″
(Amon Carter Museum, Fort Worth, TX)

A Taint in the Wind

1906, oil on canvas,
27⅛″×40″
*(Sid Richardson
Collection of Western
Art, Fort Worth, TX)*

Howl of the Weather

1906, oil on canvas,
40″×27″
(Remington Art Museum,
Ogdensburg, NY)

Following spread:

On the Southern Plains

1907, oil on canvas,
30⅛″×51⅛″
(The Metropolitan
Museum of Art, New York,
NY. Gift of Several
Gentlemen, 1911)

49

Fired On

c. 1907, oil on canvas,
27⅛″ × 40″
*(National Museum of
American Art,
Smithsonian
Institution. Gift of
William T Evans)*

The Sentinel

1907, oil on canvas, 36″×27″
(Remington Art Museum, Ogdensburg, NY)

The Fight for the Waterhole

1901, oil on canvas,
27″×40″
(*The Hogg Brothers Collection, Museum of Fine Arts, Houston, TX*)

Apache Medicine Song

1908, oil on canvas,
27⅛″×29⅞″
(Sid Richardson
Collection of Western Art,
Fort Worth, TX)

Following spread:

The Smoke Signal

1909, oil on canvas, 30½″×48½″
(Amon Carter Museum, Fort Worth, TX)

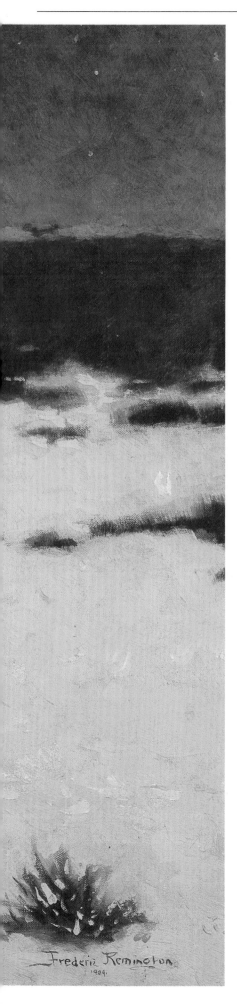

The Luckless Hunter

1909, oil on canvas, $28\frac{7}{8}'' \times 28\frac{7}{8}''$
(Sid Richardson Collection of Western Art, Fort Worth, TX)

Hauling in the Gill Net

nd, oil on canvas, 20″ × 26″
(Remington Art Museum, Ogdensburg, NY)

CHARLES MARION RUSSELL (1864-1926)

It is inevitable that the art of Frederic Remington and Charles Russell should invite comparison. Charles Russell himself made such comparisons obtusely when he would express bewilderment over Remington's national adoration and his own relative national obscurity. They did the 'same work,' he often reminded his Montana supporters.

Fortunately, there are differences between these two witnesses of the Old West. These differences permit the viewer to inspect their time and place and come away with a more encompassing view of the Old West, thanks to their varying perceptions.

Remington was a sojourner. He would develop more style in his art than the largely unschooled Russell. Remington came and went, unable to resist either the salons of the East or the saloons of the West. For Russell, the West was no part-time venture. It was not a region from which one could withdraw for refreshment. There was no going anywhere but where you were – in the West. The commitment had to be full time to have any integrity. Charlie Russell was a bona fide, hell-bent-for-leather cowboy who turned a natural drawing and painting ability into a full-time pursuit. He painted the West not only as he found it and knew it but as he wanted it to remain. There was a glimmer of the realist romantic in his conservatism. Remington painted the West as he found it, too, and as he knew it, but also as he thought it should be. He was a romantic realist. Therein lies their fundamental difference.

Remington and Russell were illustrators. Russell actually said as much: 'I am an illustrator. There are lots better ones, but some worse.' Their pictures told stories. No detail escaped their attention. They knew their horses. They knew the people indigenous to their western world. They knew the anatomy of the West.

Remington was, perhaps, the more sophisticated artist of the two. He was nearly self-taught artistically. His art training at the Yale School of Fine Arts and his classes at the Art Students

Charles Marion Russell (NYPL)

League were all too brief. He did, however, possess a better than passing knowledge of the art establishment and some historical familiarity. He approached the West from a broader, more educated perspective than Charlie Russell. And this perspective gave his late works a hint of stylistic elegance that may not have been fully realized. His life was too short.

Charlie Russell was entirely self taught. He brought to his art a less educated view of the sweep of the changing West. Nevertheless, his art was underwritten, so to speak, by a natural intelligence and wisdom. At first look, Remington and Russell painted actions seem to duplicate one another. No so. Russell's paintings had a pervasive quality that seemed to strike at the western raw nerve – a quality not often found in the Remingtons. It was the knee-jerking muscularity of the West that some say only a cowpoke could know and communicate.

It is well to point out here that personal experience or first-hand knowledge of a subject does not always generate works of art nor is personal experience a prerequisite for a work of art. In 1918, George Bellows, a painter of the American scene painted *The Murder of Edith Cavell*. Edith Louisa Cavell was a British Red Cross nurse who helped wounded Allied soldiers escape from German occupied Belgium. For this she was executed by a German firing squad during World War I. Bellows was castigated by Joseph Pennell, a widely traveled and prominent American etcher, for having had the temerity of creating a picture of an event he had not witnessed. Bellows responded with an open letter published by *The New York Times* in which he said, 'It is true, Mr Pennell, that I was not present at Miss Cavell's execution, but I've never heard that Leonardo Da Vinci had a ticket of admission to the Last Supper, either.'

In Charlie Russell's case, this was not altogether possible. Charlie Russell could not have painted the West without having been there. And the West could not have exploded from the painted canvasses of any artist with such truth and vitality short of Charlie Russell's familiarity, Only Charlie Russell's experience and temperament could have delivered it.

Charles Marion Russell was not a native of the territory he claimed as an artistic preserve. He was born in St Louis, Missouri on 19 March 1864. His family was well-to-do. They were Missourians at the time Missouri was the frontier and fur traders wandered up and down the Mississippi River. A number of Russell's forebears went further West than any white men during the early years of the nineteenth century. By the 1830s some of them had already settled in Indian country far west of St Louis, and this long before most white men dared to venture west of Missouri. The Russells were among the first to challenge the West. Charlie knew all the family history and the tales handed down about his heroic relatives. It stirred his blood and kept his imagination alive with incredible western adventures. Charlie supplemented his western mania by steeping himself in the dime novels that were flooding the country with lurid tales of western life. The writings of Bret Harte and others which spread the western experience everywhere east of the Mississippi River brought its romance ever closer to Charlie's eager and impressionable young mind. While the Russells were a sedate, educated and comfortable family living in a large, well-mannered house with carefully tended lawns and gardens, teenager Charlie Russell made himself the antithesis of such respectability. His obsession for everything western led him to assume what he believed to be the rude, even crude mannerisms of a rowdy cowboy.

Unkempt, shaggy headed, downright slovenly-looking in his contempt for civilized sociability and style, young Russell became in his own mind the persona of a rawboned, bushwacking, trailriding, cattlepunching cowhand. His parents were nonplussed by the intensity of Charlie's western interest. They attributed it all, however, to temporary adventurous fantasies, a typical schoolboy dementia that would disappear in good time. When it did, they reasoned, Charlie would go to college, from which he would enter the family business, leaving his cowboy dreamland, to the affliction of a visionary, misspent youth. Its memory would evoke gales of laughter later in life, no doubt. Mr and Mrs Russell were patient parents.

But Charles Russell was a zealot and showed no signs of giving in. He liked to draw. And he liked to model animals from wax or any other malleable material. His parents thought these activities were positively useless. Worse still, Charlie avoided school like the plague. Most of his hookey playing time was spent on the Mississippi River wharves. There he could be found in any season, in any weather, mingling with the roughneck river crowd. He trailed them from one dock to the next, in and out of every saloon. He listened wide-eyed to the wild yarns of the Old West, real or not, spun by the rough-looking cattlemen, gamblers, Indian fighters and western swashbucklers of every dimension. The St Louis riverfront of the late 1870s was a major collection point of all these swaggering characters and more who helped fire Charlie's restless determination to become one of them. They caught Charles Russell in their magical web. The hum of civilization was not for him.

Little did his parents realize, however, that Charlie was beyond 'saving.' He had developed into an incorrigible runaway trying to go West where he could be free of manners and the routine, if not boring, work ethic of American business. The last thing Charlie Russell thought he needed was a manicured lawn and a nine to five job.

The Russells, like the Remingtons, decided that what Charlie needed was discipline to bring him back into society's fold, to make him normal, happy and productive. Like young Frederic Remington, young Charles Russell was shipped off to a military academy as far from the West as

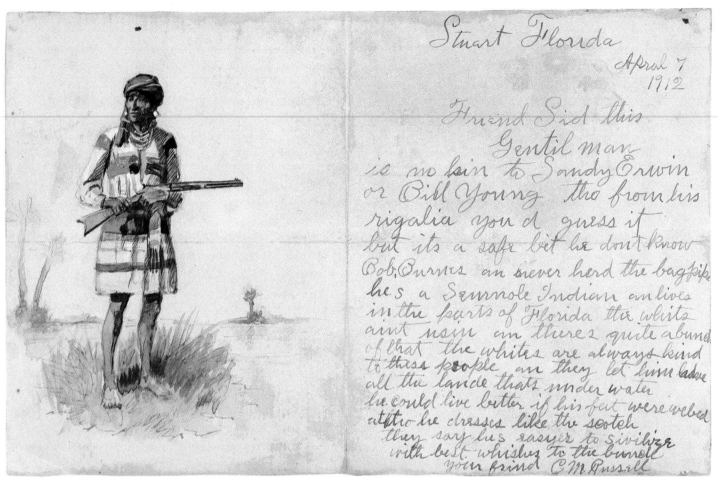

Stuart Florida
April 7
1912

Friend Sid this
Gentil man
is no kin to Sandy Erwin
or Bill Young tho from his
rigalia you d guess it
but its a safe bet he dont know
Bob Burnes an never herd the bagpipe
hes a Semnole Indian an lives
in the parts of Florida the whits
aint usin an theres quite abund
of that the whites are always kind
to these people an they let him have
all the lands thats under water
he could live better if his feat were webed
at this he dresses like the scotch
they say hes easyer to sivilize
with best whisky to the burrell
your frind C M Russell

Letter to Friend Sid (Willis) – 1912 (*Amon Carter Museum, Fort Worth, TX*)

was possible – Burlington, New Jersey. Charlie barely lasted his first term in that institution. He came home and refused to go back. Finally, after trying to improve his atrocious spelling with a private tutor and failing to interest the young man in a St Louis art school, the Russells decided to give Charlie a taste of the wild West. Arrangements were made to send the stubborn and rebellious Russell to a Montana sheep ranch in the hope that the experience of life in the raw country would settle his enthusiasm for the West forever, returning him to a more acceptable way of life.

Charlie was put in the hands of a friend of the Russell family, Pike Miller, who knew his way around the Montana Territory. Miller, a native of St Louis, was part owner of a sheep ranch in Judith Basin, an area about 200 miles due east of Helena, the principal town. In March 1880, Charlie Russell and Pike Miller boarded a Union Pacific train and headed West. They arrived some three or four weeks later at the ranch via another train – the Utah & Northern – a stage coach, and a wagon with saddle horses. Part of that time – about two weeks – was spent in Helena, a goldmining boomtown, which was to

become the capital when Montana was admitted into the Union in 1889. In 1880, however, Helena boasted a noisy population of 3000-4000, some hotels, banks, countless saloons, leathery miners, guntoting cowboys, dancing girls and others. Charlie Russell's dreamland had come to life. Here was the reality, the verification of all he read about, heard about, and imagined. Charlie was 'home.'

Charlie Russell entered Montana at the beginning of the 1880s, a decade that brought huge numbers of settlers into the area. The railroad, of course, had much to do with making the territory accessible. Good grazing lands, copper and coal made the region attractive to European immigrants. All of these things underscored by the railroad was fundamental to the enmity the Sioux, Cheyenne and other Indian nations felt for the western movement of white civilization. The annihilation of Custer at the Little Big Horn River in Montana by the Sioux and Cheyenne only four years before Charlie Russell arrived in the territory was the climax of Indian-white hostility. The battles finally ended with the defeat of Chief Joseph and the Nez Percé Nation in 1877. Still, when Charlie rode the 200-mile trail from Helena to Judith Basin for the first time there was real fear of hostile and marauding renegade Indians who were unwilling to be set down on reservations far removed from their ancestral lands. None appeared. With gold being mined in the territory, however, and hundreds of 'immigrants' moving into the area almost daily, bandits took to the trails and roads. They attacked a considerable number of overland stages which were poorly protected in a climate of ineffective law enforcement. Stagecoach hold-ups would become a fitting subject for later Russell canvasses. Meanwhile, Charlie added a six shooter to his belongings, which included a small box of watercolor paints and some brushes.

Charlie quickly became known as 'Kid' Russell around the Judith Basin. After only a couple of weeks in Helena, Kid Russell had a reputation in the town as 'that uncouth Missouri boy who came to Montana with Pike Miller.' Sixteen-year-old Kid Russell did all he could in dress and manner to pretend that he belonged to the rugged Montana country. In truth his role playing, if that is what it was, set him apart from the natives – cowboys and hotel clerks alike – many of whom were vain and caring about their dress and manner. Charlie was so disdainful of all the rules of civilized society that he paid scant attention to personal grooming. Haircombing, haircutting, clean clothes, tucked-in shirts and the like were ignored. He would have no part of them. He was free of all that in a wide open space – Montana.

In any event, Kid Russell did establish himself on arrival that he was special. He may have stood out from the crowd as a gawky, green, and impressionable youngster from 'the States,' but he could draw cowboys and horses better than anyone else in the Montana Territory. Moreover, he could model them out of clay or wax. Once in a while, he would carve them out of potatoes. These artistic skills alone excited the interest of all those hardbitten, leathery, outdoor types whose direct contact with art and artists in their immediate environment was minimal if not non-existent.

The West cast its spell over Charlie Russell. But Charlie 'Kid' Russell was his own magical being. He was a spellbinder, this 'uncouth Missouri boy,' whose power to communicate the Western experience was recognized by all those who actually lived it – the cowboys, saloonkeepers, trailmasters, teamsters and many others.

What they could all come to see was not necessarily the highly developed art and soaring visions of Russell's American contemporaries, an art thrust forward by the genius of fluid technique and craftsmanship. What comes to mind is the formidable artistic sophistication of Winslow Homer, Thomas Eakins and Howard Pyle, among others. Not to be overlooked either are the brilliantly executed and monumental historical representational actions of such early nineteenth century French painters as Françoise Gerard, Antoine Jean Gros, Theodore Gericault and Eugene Delacroix – romantics all.

What the westerner would come to see and revere in the Russell art – in such canvases as *Crippled But Still Coming* or *In Without Knocking* – was an accurate, pulsating, painted reflection of their frontier life frozen in time, on canvas – immortalized in terms of their own perception. Kid Russell was all theirs.

Young Charlie did not stay with Pike Miller very long. The sheep ranch and the life of a sheepherder held little appeal for him. He had long dreamed of being a cowboy, not a sheepman. With two Indian ponies he had bought, one to ride and one to carry his belongings, Charlie left the ranch. He had neither ample funds nor any food. After wandering around for the better part of a day and finding no employment in the sparsely populated area, Russell met up with a well-armed, well-meaning mountain man and hunter, Jake Hoover. The powerfully built and weatherbeaten Hoover had a wide and solid reputation about which Russell had no knowledge. Feeling sorry for Charlie's plight, he invited him to spend some time with him up in the mountains where he had a cabin. Charlie went with Hoover. He spent the next two years in that mountain wilderness helping Jake Hoover hunt, trap, fish and negotiate with Indians who often crossed their path. From time to time Jake and Charlie would come out of their mountain aerie and sell skins or meat. Charlie shared in some of the profits and accumulated enough to give him some feeling of independence.

In 1882 Charlie returned briefly to St Louis. He had no intention of remaining. The trip was made mainly to see his parents, most especially his mother. His parents tried everything they could to keep Charlie from heading West again.

Nothing worked. Charlie took a look around St Louis and was consumed with the urge to return to Montana. St Louis took a look at Charlie Russell and gaped at the big, raw-boned apparition that came out of the West in raggedy, slept-in clothes, a dirty misshapen felt hat on the back of his head, speaking in a drawl and lingo no one understood. Charlie had transformed himself

Paying the Fiddler

1916, oil on canvas, 24″×36″
(C M Russell Museum, Great Falls, MT)

into the rawest of rawhide cowboys, a meta-morphosis that began in his St Louis childhood. Charlie entertained friends and relatives with fancy tales about his experiences, bought some new art materials and turned westward once more.

He did not return directly to Jake Hooker's mountain cabin. Instead he took on various jobs in a great roundup of cattle in the Judith Basin. When he did return to the mountains to see Jake and retrieve his horses and other belongings he had left in Jake's care, Charlie knew that being a mountain man was not for him either. He despised the hunting and killing of animals. Down from the mountain, Charlie took on a succession of jobs, first as a 'nighthawker,' guarding cowboys' horses through the night, then as a 'nightherder,' driving cattle at night. It was in the first of these great Montana roundups in the spring of 1882 involving hundreds of cowboys and more than 10,000 heads of cattle, that Charlie's infectious enthusiasm and hard-work earned him a respected place among the tough cowpunchers. But what endeared him to this high riding bunch were the drawings and stories with which he entertained them.

By 1885, 21-year-old Charlie Russell was putting some of the more dramatic scenes to canvas with paint. His limited reputation was beginning to enlarge. One of these paintings, *Caught in the Act*, depicting a starving Indian family slaughtering a stolen steer as they were surprised by the cowboys responsible for the animal. The picture appeared three years later in the May 1888 issue of *Harper's Weekly*. Charlie had broken into print. Remington had done the same thing in *Harper's* in January. Russell's painting was editorialized as having 'truthful-ness' (i.e. realism) and 'a subject with which he is entirely familiar.' How the picture got to *Harper's* is moot. By 1888, Charlie had some wealthy cattlemen with eastern connections interested in him. Charlie, too, had been quietly nurturing some large ambitions. From time to time he would secretly send drawings eastward seeking their publication. He had little luck in the beginning.

Over the next 10 years (1885-95) Russell took on a variety of hard-riding jobs in the great roundups and cattle drives that moved beef from Montana to the trains heading to eastern stock-yards. He continued to paint and draw between jobs or whenever a mood inspired him. Much of this effort lacked polish. Otherwise, he took to the saloons and dance halls, spending his range salary as fast as he had earned it. Unemployed, by

design much of the time, Charlie would ride in and out of town with the rowdiest, loudest cowpunchers with little else on their minds but whiskey, ladies and shooting up store signs. They whooped it up in innocent fun, Montana style, until they could not sit astride their mounts.

Whenever Charlie ran out of money he would offer his art for whatever he needed, whether it was a bottle of whiskey or a dinner. The saloons were full of Charlie's art. More often than not, Charlie would simply give away his drawings and paintings to friends and amiable strangers. Little by little his art was showing up all over Montana, free of charge.

At one point he built a lopsided cabin in the Judith Basin. His family in St Louis offered to build or buy him the best ranch in the territory. Charlie resisted the offer. Here in his own cabin he hoped to stay out of the weather and have a quiet place to paint, but he built poorly and could not repair the leaky roof and drafty walls. The whole strange place was useless. Now, Kid Russell was seen as more eccentric than before, however likeable.

Charlie abandoned his cabin. He floated around, sharing cover with other cowboys or renting a room in a cheap lodging house in town. Meanwhile, the whole region had become rich with cattle and congested with incoming settlers. The law was invisible, and this lawless vacuum was infested with horse thieves, cattle rustlers, highwaymen, murderers, con men, gamblers and prostitutes. Gunfights were commonplace. Robberies were routine. Cowboy vigilantes meted out their own justice, usually swift, and invariably lethal – a rope on the nearest tree or a shot in the head. There were still problems with Indians, chiefly Crows. Although the Indian Wars had long since ended formal hostilities between red and white men, cattle drives across Indian reservations infuriated the Crows and led to serious confrontations. All these events formed the substance of everything Charlie Russell tried to save pictorially as the relentless march of civilization began to push them all into the twentieth century.

Every so often Russell went back to St Louis to buy art materials and visit with his family. He always returned to Montana quickly. In the late 1880s his reputation was great enough that he received offers from wealthy Montanans wanting to send him back East to a good art school to refine his raw talent. Charlie must have thought that any polish would ruin him and his art. He turned down the opportunity along with an offer

Letter to Friend Sid (Willis) – 1914 (*Amon Carter Museum, Fort Worth, TX*)

to study in Europe. Some of these wealthy Montanans took his paintings to Chicago and had them reproduced in portfolios for sale back home. None of this seemed to move Charlie outwardly. He surely did not become rich on their sale. Russell shrank from these manifestations of civilization, preferring his freewheeling cowpunching lifestyle, his friendship with back trail characters like Jake Hoover and the Blackfoot Indians with whom he lived for a time as a tribal brother. This later experience resulted in a group of small, sensitive and brilliant watercolors of Indian life. Inwardly, Charlie was torn between life as a cowboy and his compulsion to paint seriously. By 1896, Charlie had seen some of his drawings published regionally to illustrate texts about the West.

During the mid 1890s, Russell moved around Montana, now a state, painting in places like Great Falls, Chinook and Cascade. Little did he realize it but at a mature 30 he was settling rapidly into a lifetime occupation. Any doubts he may have had regarding a professional art career were dispelled in 1896 when he met and married

Nancy Cooper. The taming of Kid Russell began then, setting him firmly on the track of art.

Charlie began to work long hours at his art. Between 1896 and 1900, the Russells found small success locally in the sale or reproduction of Charlie's pictures. Some of these pictures found their way to New York where they were published in such magazines as *Field and Stream* and *Recreation*. But Charlie was not being paid a great deal for this. Charlie had received an inheritance from his mother's modest estate – she had died in 1895 – and his father appeared with an offer to set the struggling couple up in a decent house in Great Falls. Charlie was unsure about such domestic responsibility.

As hard as he worked at his painting and drawing, which was improving with remarkable speed, he did not like surrendering altogether his trips to the saloons with his cowboy cronies. But give it up he did. And in the end, thanks to the elder Russell, Charlie and Nancy had a big house in Great Falls to which they added a log cabin studio a few years later.

By 1903, Nancy had taken over the job of

Signal Smoke

1914, oil on canvas,
22½″×35″
*(C M Russell Museum,
Great Falls, MT)*

When Ignorance is Bliss

1910, watercolour,
28"×22"
*(Duquesne Club,
Pittsburgh, PA)*

selling Charlie's art. Old friends and wealthy merchants Ben Roberts and Charles Schatzlein promoted the Russell name. Charlie's work was seen at the great Louisiana Purchase Exposition Fair in St Louis in 1903. There were selling trips to New York and California. Altogether, these excursions helped to enhance Charlie's fame beyond Montana. Book and magazine illustrating and writing commissions came tumbling in. People wanted to know about the West from one who had lived the rugged western life. They wanted the authenticity. Tiffany and Company in New York began to sell some of his sculpture cast in bronze. Charlie himself began writing illustrated letters to all of his friends while on these jaunts. The letters themselves, his home-spun observations and their graphic illumina-tions, were works of art. *Outing* magazine contracted with him to write and illustrate his western experience. These eventually became

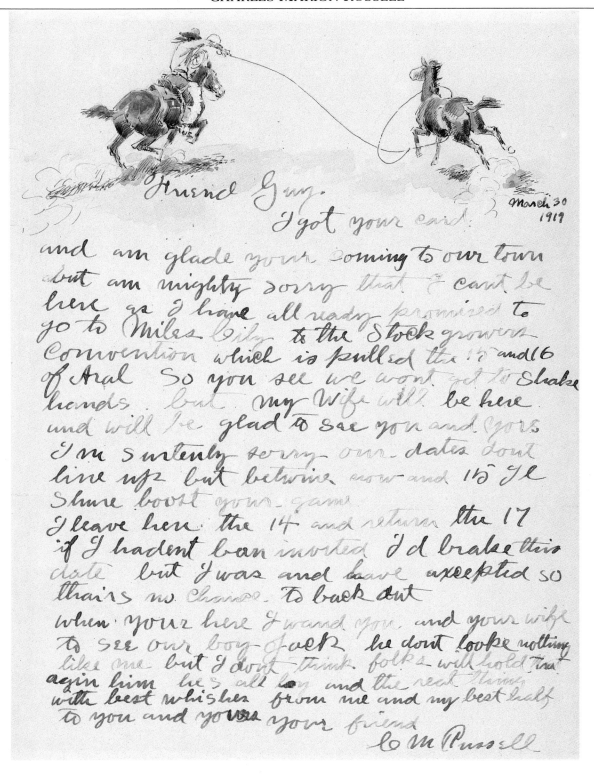

Letter to Friend Guy (Wendlick) – 1919 (*Amon Carter Museum, Fort Worth, TX*)

known as the 'Rawhide Rawlins' stories. They were published in book form in 1921. There were illustrations and writing projects for *McClure's* magazine and others. Printing houses bought his art to be reproduced on calendars.

In 1911, Charles Marion Russell reached out to a greater America with his first one-man exhibition in Manhattan. By 1920, Russell paintings were being sold for large sums, the least of which was about $10,000.

Yet, with all the riches, recognition and honors that came to him the last six years of his life Charlie never lost sight of his romance with the West, albeit a West now gone, and with the remembrance of its natural purity. He spent a lifetime fixing that image eternally in his art.

'The biggest part of the Rocky Mountains,' he wrote, 'still belongs to God.'

Charles Marion Russell died 24 October 1926, in Great Falls, Montana.

When Guns Speak, Death Settles Dispute

nd, oil on canvas, 24⅛″ × 36⅛″ (*Thomas Gilcrease Institute, Tulsa, OK*)

The Silk Robe

c. 1890, oil on canvas, 27⅝″ × 39⅛″
(*Amon Carter Museum, Fort Worth, TX*)

Sioux Torturing a Blackfoot Brave

1891, watercolor, 15″×20¼″
(Buffalo Bill Historical Center, Cody, WY)

The Defiant Culprit

1895, oil on masonite panel, 18½″ × 24¾″
(Sid Richardson Collection of Western Art, Fort Worth, TX)

The Herd Quitter

*1897, oil on canvas,
20″×31″
(Montana Historical
Society, Helena, MT. Gift
of Colonel Wallis
Huidekoper)*

When Cowboys Get In Trouble

1899, oil on canvas,
24″×36″
(Sid Richardson
Collection of Western Art,
Fort Worth, TX)

Lake McDonald

c. 1901, oil on board,
9¾″×14″
(Amon Carter Museum, Fort
Worth, TX)

The Strenuous Life

1901, oil on canvas,
36″×23″
(Thomas Gilcrease
Institute, Tulsa, OK)

The Buffalo Hunt
1901, oil on canvas,
24⅛″ × 36⅛″
(Sid Richardson
Collection of Western Art,
Fort Worth, TX)

Trouble Hunters

1902, oil on canvas,
22″×29⅛″
(Sid Richardson Collection
of Western Art, Fort Worth,
TX)

The Wounded Buffalo

1909, oil on canvas,
19⅞″×30⅛″
*(Sid Richardson Collection of
Western Art, Fort Worth, TX)*

In Without Knocking

1909, oil on canvas,
20⅛″×29⅞″
(*Amon Carter Museum,
Fort Worth, TX*)

The Jerkline

1912, oil on canvas,
24″×30″
(C M Russell Museum,
Great Falls, MT)

Smokin' 'em Out

1912, oil on linen, 29¼″ × 32½″
(Wichita Art Museum, Wichita, KS. M C Naftzager Collection)

The Innocent Allies

1912, oil on canvas,
24″×36″
(*Thomas Gilcrease
Institute, Tulsa, OK*)

**Lewis and Clark
Meeting the Flatheads
at Ross' Hole**

1912, oil mural,
25′×12′
*(Montana Historical
Society, Helena, MT)*

The Round Up #2

c. 1913, oil on canvas, 25″×49″
(Montana Historical Society, Helena, MT. Mackay Collection)

When Shadows Hint Death

1915, oil on canvas,
30″×40″
*(Duquesne Club,
Pittsburgh, PA)*

The Price of His Hide

1915, oil on canvas,
24⅛″×36⅛″
(Amon Carter Museum,
Fort Worth, TX)

**Loops and Swift Horses
Are Surer than Lead**

1916, oil on canvas,
29″×47½″
(Amon Carter Museum,
Fort Worth, TX)

Where Tracks Spell Meat

1916, oil on canvas,
31½″×49½″
*(Thomas Gilcrease
Institute, Tulsa, OK)*

Following spread:

Salute to the Robe Trade

1920, oil on canvas,
29″×47″
*(Thomas Gilcrease
Institute, Tulsa, OK)*

Russell on Redbird

1906, watercolor, 12″ × 8¾″ (C M Russell Museum, Great Falls, MT)

Friar Tuck

c. 1910, bronze, 7½″ × 7½″ × 3½″ (C M Russell Museum, Great Falls, MT)

Bear on Log

c. 1912, silver casting, 5⅜″×7″×4½″ (*C M Russell Museum, Great Falls, MT*)

Standing Buffalo

1901, bronze, 7″ × 7½″ × 4¾″ (C M Russell Museum, Great Falls, MT)

Bucking Bronco

1905, bronze, 5¾″ × 4½″ × 3″ (*C M Russell Museum, Great Falls, MT*)

Piegan Maiden

c. 1910, bronze, 10¼″ × 6½″ × 5½″ (C M Russell Museum, Great Falls, MT)

Index of Artworks

Acknowledgements

The author and the publishers would like to thank the following people who have helped in the preparation of this book:
Mike Rose, who designed it;
Elizabeth Montgomery, who edited it;
Sheila Byrd, who did the picture research.